DARKNESS AND LIGHT

THE POETRY OF LIFE

R. RADHAKRISHNAN

Dedicated

To

GANESHA

&

R. Ramamurthy, my father

Contents

Contents

Foreword

Life is mix, of good and bad. We are ourselves a mix of evil and goodness. All humans are.

There is darkness and light everywhere, one cannot exist without the other.

Inside us too there is good and bad, light and dark. Situations trigger emotions and these can be happiness, sadness, anger, frustration or any of the emotions we feel.

Poetry is an expression of these emotions in words.

Our life is made up of good moments and bad moments and our reactions to the situations defines us.

Poetry is an expression of feelings, thoughts, emotions. An outpouring of your reaction to situations.

In this small volume I share my emotions especially those triggered by the pandemic which has tested us so sorely and brought out the best and worst in us.

I hope you can relate to at least a few of these poems of mine.

I would love to have your feedback on these poems of mine. You can email me at krishnanrr2622@gmail.com.

My blog site is https://thepassageofmind.wordpress.com/

R. Radhakrishnan

Cochin, Kerala.

1. The book of Darkness

Darkness

2. Shadow in my Soul

In the darkness
There is no light
Shadows in grey
A deeper darkness
Swirls within.
The canopy above
Of a moonless night

The air is still
You sit and doze
As a mind numbs.
The moon flickers
You hope but fear
Silence stretches
The dawn is still
Far away, not near.
Fear holds your hand
Walking beside
Happiness is trending
We wear our masks
Cloak the despair.
Sadness is my shadow
Dull ache my friend
My eyes tell the tale
Of a soul lost
In the darkness of time.
Reflections regrets
Is a waste
Of energy and hope
I struggle mired
Swamped by thoughts.
The flickering lamps
The wavery light
The rise of hope
The crash of reality

Shadows come to life.
No one to share
The darkness within
It is my own
My very own
Fattened, fed in the mind.

3. Virus Views

High up in Ivory towers
Sitting in protected bowers
Watching with tinted eyes
While the world below cries
The air is pure I say
Save the world this way
Fear makes me blind
I see only the rind
Rotted fruit within
Masses bone and skin
Toil struggle and still
Empty bellies to fill
Work from home
Stop not to roam
Eyes glitter speak
Spirits grow weak
All I see are masks,
Oblivious to tasks
Beggar on the street
Kids with fleet feet
Cobbler on the corner
The tattooed foreigner
Begone and away

On fort walls only sea spray
Roads blank and forlorn
Vehicle where is your horn?
Life stands still
Tapestry yet to fill
The temple bells are still
Life flows on still
Clouds gather and swirl
Thoughts are a whirl
The darkness gathers
Over the land of our fathers
What about our mothers?
But then who bothers
The roads full of gaggle
Walking home to a fraggle
The ways are hard
Moving on a shard
Filling bellies on charity
The virus has no clarity
It reaches up high
There is no place to fly…

4. MIGRANT

I have seen death strike sometimes sudden and sometimes lingering reluctant to take.

When it is sudden it is always a shock as it is unexpected.

Today a migrant worker died, a slab slid high up on a new building trapping him between an iron rod and the slab as he hung outside on the scaffolding.

We watched him die.

It was traumatic and brought home a fundamental truth that we all are transient.

A friend and classmate sent a link to his podcast and the first one was on the need to share the love. His message was simple, sweet, and short. Please tell the people in your life that you love them.

Simple yes, but most of us are so busy with the inanities of life that we forget. It is mostly the men who do this in India. They are so busy climbing up the career path or social ladder that they ignore this. They always think they will make it up later but that day may not ever come.

We look at migrants suspiciously, forgetting that many of us have been migrants at some time or the other

We look down on these people and pass derogatory remarks and say he is not even from our country he is from a neighbouring country.

But today I realized it did not matter where he is from. He is a human, like me.

He has come because of the need to live, because of his responsibility to his loved ones. He has not come to make life hard for me. He has come to make life easy for me by doing work I will not do. He has come as he has a hard life and he wants to work and live with dignity.

He probably has a family he loves, he probably never told them what they meant to him. Now he never can.

His origin does not matter, his language does not matter, his religion does not matter. All that matters is that he was a human striving for a better life.

5. A Migrant's Death

It hung swaying
The arms flapped
The head lolled
Puppet without strings.
Load on his back
He hung there
In pain
Searching help
In vain.
Family, food
Education, home
Children, parents
Siblings, marriage
Life's load.
A long road
A strange place
A better life
Dreams he had
Reality struck today.
High up
He worked
A slide
Slab of stone

On his back.
Humans watched
No one helped
Life squeezed
In pain
Slipped out.
In peace
He hung
Swaying gently.
They cut him down
Wailings afar.
Life went on
Just a migrant
Too poor
To matter.

6. A time of loss

The leaves are still,
The trees don't sway
The world is waiting
An eerie calm around
The sun sinks slowly
Every breath is pleasure
Who knows when it ends?
Men in arrogant Hubris
Owned the world
Ravaged the land
Nature was patient
She cajoled, she warned
Humanity was lost
The scourge unleashed
In droves they died
Like flies they dropped
Rich men, poor men
Great men, little men
The young and the old
Friends gone without a word
Leaving behind shocked fear
Boundaries make no sense
The invisible one strikes

High and low
In a Random flow.
I sit in numbness
I sit struck dumb
I have no thoughts
In a bereft bereaved mind
I mourn for friends
I mourn for the loss
Frustration fuels anger
Helpless I wait
For the next blow to fall
I hold to my heart
Friends and memories
Yesterday was light
Laughter in the sun bright
As darkness falls on my land
I search my soul and mind
I yearn for the days of old
Friends whose hands I can hold.

7. Darkness

I fear the darkness
Inside and insidious
Gnawing away
Eroding the mind
The light struggles
Trapped in a corner
Anger rises
The darkness feeds
It is bright daylight
Yet the shadows grow
They numb my sense
The heart dreads
The mind flitters
Round and around
In dark alleys
Of shadowy thoughts
I give up the battle
Some days are like that
I pick up my pen
And shadows drip
Dark ink forms my words
Thoughts let out
Some relief from the dark

The light is lit as a spark.

8. A slow death

Lost in the dark
The devil is in me
Turbulence and trials
Emotions wreck
Relations break
Links forged weak
The mind numbs
The heart breaks
Woman I wish
You happiness
I wish you joy
Watch me die
Bit by bit
Chip away at my heart
Forget laughter
It has been long
Since I smiled.

9. Rage

The madness is on me
The darkness of the soul
The anger of loss
The fear of loneliness
The body falters
The mind drifts
Yesterdays are missed
The present is a misery
Existence without aim
The indolence of wait

The rage is there
Reined in tight
Fires burning my inside
The smile is a mask
Of the snarl within
The growls of rage
Silent screams
Of a bereft mind
A heart unwanted
Disposed after need
The rage builds up
I dam it tight
It rages to reach
The flailing tongue
Decades together
A waste of my life.

10. The Broken Mind

The mind is dark
In complex knots
Pathways blurred
Meandering in dark
Heart beats in fear
No one is near
Lost that is dear
Twist and turn
Mind hold terror
In fetters grim
Dark and foreboding
Reality fades
Mind awakes
In darkness
Is peace
End it
Soon.

11. The lost mind

Angst inside
Dullness death
Mind mindless
Eyes no sight
Heart in pain
Emotions churn
Fear fuels despair
Maze all around
Trapped mind frets
Morning is a haze
Rote is king
Body moves
Without mind
I am lost.

12. The book of Light

Light

13. Healing

The mind breaks
Loss unbearable
Heart poundS
In fits and starts
Tears flow unheeded
Darkness despair
All pervading
A light gleams
Faint yet strong
A glimmer
Of Hope
Friends gather
Humans touch
Soft hands gentle
The Broken mind
Ignites reunites

14. Once upon a time

Once upon a time
When I was slim
And yes, a little dim
Care free child
Playful a little wild
The child is lost
Adults pay a cost
The years take a toll
Often in ways droll
Twists and turns
As destiny churns
The mind is jaded
The memory faded
Life is a circle round
Old mates are found
Gone are adult fears
As the child reappears
Once upon a time
Once more…

15. Laughing away our fears

It is out there, the enemy
Of life, laughter and love
It grips the heart with fear
It muddles the mind in rage
But I am amidst my friends
Surrounded by those I love
We laugh at silly stuff
We never feel our age
We look fear in the eye
There is misery in loss
The heart mourns in tears
But we rally round
Together we will hold
We will laugh all we can
We will laugh our fears away.

16. Abide my friend

The sun sets in a rush
Twilight descends in a hush.
Death stalks in the air
Catching one unaware.
It is going to be a long night
Full of worry anger and fright
The darkness lies on the land
Threatening in a multiple strand.
Air hangs still, the wait is long
Need to keep our faith strong
This darkness will also end
The Sun, its light will send
We will walk together old friend
This too shall pass and end.
Together, we will watch that dawn
A Golden light falling on the lawn
We will clasp our hands
We will come from all the lands.
From the East, from the West
North and South, full of Zest
We will sit together break bread
We will catch up our life's thread
One day soon this nightmare will end

Till then abide and await my friend.

17. Hope

Silences awake
Soul within
Mind meanders
Random thoughts
Stillness seeps
Sleeping soul
Focused mind
Opened eyes
Cloister cacophony
Clutter mind
Round round
Aimless circles

Thoughts jump
Heart fears
Day follows
Night comes
Dawn dispels
Dark mind
Rays warm
On my face
Eyes closed
Step forward
Life awaits
Leap ahead!

18. Night

Nights warm
Sleep oblivion
Rain pattering
A lullaby
Dreams do die
Reality a pain
Morning dull
Aching head
Life floats around
A stagnant me
Left behind
Unwanted
Heart beats
Mind swirls
Eyes see
Darkness
Comes the knight
Steed of darkness
Relief and Rescue
A Good night

19. Happiness and Joy

Happiness and Joy
Rain on the roof
Puddles on the ground
Feeling in the mind.
Breeze on face
Hum of tyres
Rustle of leaves
Heartbeats.
Smell of Earth
Touch your love
Hold her close
Breath in her hair.
Flowers in bloom
Child at play
Crow on the tree
Grinning at me.
Squirrels chattering
Love of a dog
Friends lost
Meet again.
Its yesterday
Child again
Siblings speak

A little touch
Kindred look
Happiness and Joy
Perception in the mind.

20. KARNA

21. KARNA and INDRA

I walked to meet the dawn
Golden rays on my brow
The war on the horizon
The brothers five in my sight
Years of slights, humiliation
Time now to pay in full.
My bow was stringed
Arrows sharp and straight
The day had come
Retribution!
The Sun spoke in my mind
Retribution and revenge
Come around in circles
But I was firm for a fight.
An old man on the steps
Asking for alms in my way
My armour and earrings
He wanted my life in charity.
Sun whispering in my mind
Beware, Indra the sneak
Seeking favour for his son.
I laughed at Indra,
King of gods

Supplicant for his Archer son
My arrows still sheathed
I had already won!
I tore my armour,
Cut my earrings
Indra stood in shame
As they dropped in his hands
His hands red in my blood.
Pain ignored; my spirit soared
Smiling, I bowed my head
You have made me immortal
Oh, Indra lord of the heavens.
The shaft struck him true
He stood his glory dim
Guilty and shamed
He offered me a trade.
Ask me a boon oh Karna
I laughed at that
I gave freely what you asked
I gave you alms not a price.
Guilt, anger and shame
He shivered at his deed
I give you a boon Karna
My Vajra, the thunderbolt.
I did not seek it
I did not want it
I had faith

In me and my arms.
But yet he was Indra
Lord of the heavens
I gave him the gift
Of redemption.
Indra laid the weapon in my hands
Unhappy and reluctant
Worried in his giving,
He still feared for his son.
Use it wisely, but only once
Indra was a miser still
His heart not in the giving
He set conditions and curbs.
I laughed at him
They called me low born
I knew not my mother
I knew not my father.
But my heart was true
My spirit still strong
I was a warrior true
Indra shamed sneaked away.

22. Karna and Kunti

I stood in the light
The dark in me alight
Small she stood straight
Red eyes on my face
My son, she whispered
My sin, I heard.
Krishna came too late
The truth so frightening
She now stood before me
My heart exulted; mind numb
My mother, burden and sorrow.
Speech fled, thought died
Anger and sadness mingled
Harsh words I spoke
Love burst; regret flamed
I took that small hand.
She gripped with strength
Hugged me to her heart
Tears washed my anger
Leaving love saddened
Truth is bitter, truth is anguish.
She tempted me
Brothers, family, kingdom, wife

Respect, repute, fame and glory
I smiled, I was her son too
Firm would I be, in friendship
I put her away gently
I knew now my worth
A life was all I could give
But I gave her four lives
One would I take, I said
But in my heart, I knew
I was my own enemy
He was my brother
I could not take, only give
One life I had, that I would give
To my friend, my mother
I had nothing else to give.

23. Karna's Death

The wheel was in the rut
All I did would not avail
But yet I strained
All my life was a rut
But yet I abide
Struggle to survive
I would not surrender
To fate and destiny
To the end
To the end of days.
My brother stood
Bow in his hand,
Hate in his eyes
I bent my head
Shamed even at end
He set the arrow
His hand shook
I looked up
At Krishna's eyes
Compassionate smiling
My heart was filled
Love and peace
My search was to end

My brother's bow snapped
I watched death come
I smiled offered myself
In peace I lay
Unbroken unbent.

24. Karna's Soul

The soul shed its mortal coil
Broke the bonds that drag
It was twilight, harbinger of night
Yet I lingered, not fully free
Above that ground of death
Barren land drenched in blood
The body lay headless
Strong limbs asprawl
The head unblinking watched
Jackals tore the entrails
I felt not the pain
It was me for so long
Striding in strength
Alive across this land
My arms were strong
My shoulders broad
Benign Sun, my father
Watched as I grew
In strength and fame
And yet I felt that pain
A yearning to belong.
She came then, iron lady
Small, hard, emotions in thrall

She took my head in her arms
She sat forlorn in that field
My blood on her hands
She held the rotting flesh to her
She pulled that broken body
Hugged it like she would never let go
I was the soul, undying spirit
I felt not the bonds of Earth
And yet I felt her pain
They came together then
My brothers unknown
Hesitant with dragging steps
They watched their mother
Wail and weep over me
Their shattered faces
Distressed eyes, let me know
The pain they felt and the guilt
The Archer sat at my feet
His head drooped and he sobbed
My soul felt that cry of pain
The others sobbed in grief
I could but watch their pain
I could share the sorrow
At last, I knew myself
It was time for me to go.

Author Picture

R. Radhakrishnan

AUTHOR PICTURE

Feedback

Thank you for buying and reading this book. I would love to hear from you. my email id is krishnanrr2622@gmail.com. Drop me a line and I will respond.

My facebook author page is R. Radhakrishnan, check it our to preview my other writings.

9 798886 841299